T0129937

BALANCED CHRISTIAN HOME

BENJAMIN MITTAPALLI

WESTBOW
P R E S S
A DIVISION OF THOMAS NELSON

WestBow Press books may be ordered through booksellers or by contacting:

WestBow Press
A Division of Thomas Nelson
1663 Liberty Drive
Bloomington, IN 47403
www.westbowpress.com
1-(866) 928-1240

ISBN: 978-1-4497-1461-1 (sc)
ISBN: 978-1-4497-1462-8 (e)

Library of Congress Control Number: 2011924772

Printed in the United States of America

WestBow Press rev. date: 6/16/2011

This book is dedicated for the glory of God to my wonderful parents, Drs. Praveen Kumar and Leela Mittapalli, who dedicated me to the service of the Lord while I was still in my mother's womb.

As for me and my house, we will serve the LORD.

(Joshua 24:15).

Psalm 127

[1]Unless the LORD builds the house,
They labor in vain who build it;
Unless the LORD guards the city,
The watchman keeps awake in vain.
[2]It is vain for you to rise up early,
To retire late,
To eat the bread of painful labors;
For He gives to His beloved even in his sleep.
[3]Behold, children are a gift of the LORD,
The fruit of the womb is a reward.
[4]Like arrows in the hand of a warrior,
So are the children of one's youth.
[5]How blessed is the man whose quiver is full of them;
They will not be ashamed
When they speak with their enemies in the gate.

CONTENTS

1. Introduction

Christian life is bi-directional, with vertical and horizontal relationships, where the vertical relationship is with God and the horizontal relationship is with people around us. The cross also signifies these vertical and horizontal aspects. A Christian should have vertical and horizontal relationships in his or her daily life. Both vertical and horizontal relationships, when properly maintained, make up a balanced Christian life.

Whether you are single or married, or parent or grandparent, it is important to understand, from the Word of God, what it means to live like a Christian and make a Christian home. Everybody has a home. Even singles have homes—sometimes alone, sometimes with parents and siblings. If you live singly, or share an apartment with friends, you still live in a home where you feel like going to at the end of the day to rest. Every person should understand the importance of a Christian home.

In some places (such as churches), wonderful sermons are preached about horizontal relationships, concentrating on how to live on this Earth, how to love others, and how to deal with other people. In some other places, the preaching is about vertical relationships, concentrating on how to maintain a relationship with God, not on having a good relationship with fellow believers. We have to maintain balance and give importance to both vertical and horizontal relationships.

You might say, "I have a good relationship with God, but it is getting hard for me to relate with people," or "I have a clear conscience with God, but I cannot have a clear conscience with people." God is the one who established the concept of relationships and family; He is the one who established the home; there was a purpose for Him to give both the vertical and horizontal relationships.

In our further study, we will be looking into the horizontal relationships while the vertical relationship is the prominent one. Many psychologists and counselors concentrate only on how to relate with people; there are many books on this subject. The purpose of *Balanced Christian Home* is to look at the Word of God and learn what the Bible has to say about Christian living.

Our first and foremost priority is to have a vertical relationship with God. If we have no vertical relationship, no matter how good our horizontal relationships may be, it has no significant value in the sight of God. If we have a vertical relationship, it has to be reflected horizontally. If it is not reflected horizontally, it means there is an issue. We have to examine our lives and see how to live in this world as a balanced Christian, cultivating a practical Christian home.

It is important for us to have a realization of our sinful nature, and that Christ alone can forgive us our sins when we repent and ask for forgiveness. If you do not have that experience of salvation, it is vital you consider taking this first step toward Christian living. Later, take the opportunity to share the importance of salvation and gospel with your family members. As mentioned in Acts 16:31, "Believe in the Lord Jesus, and you will be saved, you and your household." Your household members will start noticing your changed life and, as a result, will be drawn to Christ. Acts 16 records how Lydia was first saved and then influenced her family members. Jailor, mentioned in the same chapter, influenced his whole family to be saved and be baptized. Joshua 24:15 says, "As for me and my house, we will serve the Lord."

What did God tell Noah when he was supposed to build an ark? Genesis 7:1 says, "Enter the ark, you and all your household, for you alone I have seen to be righteous before Me in this time." God told Noah to take his whole family along with him into the ark. From a spiritual perspective, entering into the ark means to be saved from destruction. After the floods, all humans died, except Noah's family, who were saved. It was Noah's responsibility, as the head of the family, to bring his family members into the ark and be saved. Genesis 7:7 says, "Then Noah and his sons and his wife and his sons' wives with him entered the ark because of the water of the flood." Look at the sequence how they entered into the ark. Noah's son's wives followed their husbands but did not influence them otherwise. When the head of the family is a man of God, he will influence his whole family, and the family members obey the man of God. Verse 1 tells of God's command to Noah, and in verse 7, we see the obedience to God's command.

My prayer as you read this book is that God would speak to you afresh through His Scriptures to live a practical Christian life where we will be able to balance our relationships for His glory.

2. HOUSE OR HOME?

Unless the LORD builds the house, they labor in vain who build it (Psalm 127:1).

There are two builders mentioned—the LORD, who is the master builder, and people, who are the other builders. "Other" does not mean construction workers, but household members. The LORD is the chief architect. "For every house is built by someone, but the builder of all things is God (Hebrews 3:4)." The LORD and His people are involved in bringing up a structure for the home. The word "house" in original Hebrew is "bayeth," which is translated as house, family, home, and household. It is important to understand the meaning of "home" from a biblical perspective in order to maintain good relationships with each other.

What is the difference between a house and a home?
A house is a physical structure; and a home is a place with people where love is expressed, and concerns are shared with each other.

In the English language, the words "house" and "home" have different meanings. A house is not a home until there are people in it. An empty

5

house cannot be called a home. All of us would like to go back to our own "home sweet home" and relax comfortably. A house is a physical structure, while a home is a place where love is expressed and concerns are shared with each other.

Acronym of H-O-M-E

H: Honesty/Hospitality
A truthful witness gives honest testimony, but a false witness tells lies. (Proverbs 12:17)
Offer hospitality to one another without grumbling. (1 Peter 4:9)

O: Order
Set your house in order (Isaiah 38:1)

M: Merciful
Blessed are the merciful, for they will be shown mercy. (Matthew 5:7)

E: Encouragement/Exhortation
Encourage one another and build each other up. (1 Thessalonians 5:11)
Until I come, give attention to the public reading of Scripture, to exhortation and teaching. (1 Timothy 4:13)

Honesty

A truthful witness gives honest testimony, but a false witness tells lies. (Proverbs 12:17)

April 30 is known as National Honesty Day. But for a Christian, every day should be an "honesty day." An important component that makes up a home is honesty, between husband and wife, or between children and parents. To be honest is to be truthful and frank. A Christian home requires honesty, which is important in our relationships. Be honest; do good and not evil deeds. Honesty is something often done with words. If you speak the truth, you are being honest. If you are always ready in your mind to tell truth and not lies, you will show honesty in your words and deeds.

Hospitality

Be hospitable to one another without complaint. We ought therefore to show hospitality to such men so that we may work together for the truth (1 Peter 4:9; 3 John 1:8).

The members of a Christian home should always show hospitality by opening their home to welcome others in fellowship. The original Greek word for "hospitality" is *"philoxenos,"* which means "to be generous to guests." The good quality of hospitality will be passed on from parents to children. It need not be taught. The children will learn from their parents—who are hospitable and never murmur or grumble when guests visit their house. Receiving people and showing hospitality enables us to show our faith in works, being not only the hearers but the doers of the Word. Romans 12:13 and Hebrews 13:2 also mention the important Christian virtue of being hospitable to the saints as well as strangers, who could be angels sent by God.

Order

In those days, Hezekiah became mortally ill and Isaiah the prophet the son of Amoz came to him and said to him, "Thus says the LORD, 'Set your house in order, for you shall die and not live'" (Isaiah 38:1).

King Hezekiah was going to die, and he was told so by the prophet, Isaiah, who told him to "set his house in order." See how important setting one's house in order is! Just before death, Hezekiah was told to set his house in order. It does not mean to physically clean the house and set things in order. Yes, we have to physically keep our houses clean and in order; otherwise, a messy house will result in irritation and shouting in the household. However, much more than that, the household members have to be set in order. Be watchful what kinds of "things" are within the house, such as the thoughts being brought into the house, or things being taken away, in terms of morality and thinking. Set your house in order.

The Lord is the master builder, and those who are building the house (household members) are very much responsible for putting things in order. We have to learn from the Word of God how we can keep our houses in order. We may not have perfect homes, although some may be close to perfection, but every house will have its strengths and weaknesses. We have to keep everything in order and aim toward perfection. The adults of the house - husband and wife, or father and mother are responsible for keeping a house in order.

Merciful

Blessed are the merciful, for they will be shown mercy

(Matthew 5:7).

It does not say to first receive mercy and then be merciful to others. It says show mercy and you will be shown mercy. The more merciful you are, the more merciful God will be toward you. The more merciful you are, the more merciful others will be toward you. It is a case of give and take. To be merciful means to show compassion and help those in need.

The Greek word for "mercy" is *"eleos,"* which, roughly translated, means "kindness or goodwill toward the miserable and the afflicted, joined with a desire to help them." God showed that mercy toward men in offering and providing salvation by Christ. God had compassion and kindness toward us, even though we deserve the punishment for our sins. By enabling His only Son Jesus Christ to take up that punishment on our behalf, we can have eternal life. We should also show compassion and kindness to others so that the love of God is visible in our lives within our homes and society around us.

Encouragement/Exhortation

Therefore, encourage one another and build up one another, just as you also are doing ... just as you know how we were exhorting and encouraging and imploring each one of you as a father would his own children (1 Thessalonians 5:11; 2:11).

How should fathers deal with their own children? By encouraging, comforting, and urging them to live lives worthy of God. The family members of a Christian home should encourage as well as exhort one another. If a family member does well, encourage. If someone does something wrong, exhort with words to maintain discipline.

In the Bible, Barnabas (whose name means "son of encouragement and exhortation") was a man of God who is mentioned in the book of Acts. He lived up to his name in encouraging and exhorting many people, including the apostle Paul. Barnabas was responsible for building up Paul and was bold in taking and introducing Paul to Jesus' disciples. God ultimately used Paul for His glory.

3. SINGLES

If you are a single, this book will help you prepare for your future and learn how your future home should be developed. There is no better time than now to start praying for a good life partner. It does not matter if you are too young; once you know the importance of marriage, it is important to start praying for the partner that God has chosen for you, so that He will reveal the person in His time. God has planned the best for you; your life partner, who is somewhere in the world, has already been created by God, and God will make His will clear when you fully depend on Him. It is always better to pray to know God's will for your future rather than repenting later, saying, "Oh, I should have known God's will."

The Bible started with two single people: Adam and Eve. Family life starts with two singles coming together in marriage. Never think that a topic such as "home" is not for singles to discuss and is set aside for married people only. Home belongs to everybody; and everybody belongs to a home.

Then the LORD God said, "It is not good for the man to be alone; I will make him a helper suitable for him" (Genesis 2:18). You might have heard this verse quoted during weddings. God said, "It is not good for the man to be alone." God knows what is good and not good for us. God, at that particular stipulated point in time, thought that it was not good for man to be alone. Moreover, God said, "I will create a suitable helper." Who knows what is good for a man ... for who can tell man. If no one knows what will happen, who can tell him when it will happen? (Ecclesiastes 6:12; 8:7)

Many times we wonder about our future; we try to make our own decisions. God knows what is best for us. God, in His own time, brought a suitable helper to Adam. The LORD God fashioned into the woman … and brought her to the man (Genesis 2:22).

Many times, we use the word "fashion" in a wrong sense. When God created Eve, He "fashioned" her from Adam's rib and brought her to Adam. God thought it was not good for a man to be alone and brought a woman to the man. God knows and brings the right person into your life at the right time. We just have to pray and depend upon Him. Just keep praying to know the Lord's perfect will. If you depend upon God, God will show you your suitable helpmate, who was created in the image of God. You just have to wait on the Lord to know who that person is.

Apostle Paul says, "If they do not have self-control, let them marry; for it is better to marry than to burn with passion" (1 Corinthians 7:9). He who finds a wife finds a good thing, and obtains favor from the LORD (Proverbs 18:22).

When God created human beings—male and female—he brought them together. Because it is from the Lord, and it is God who brings people together, and He has a plan for bringing two people together in marriage. We see in the case of Adam and Eve that God brought Eve to Adam. God brings or shows you your right mate. Maybe that person is nearby or far away. God brings two people together in marriage.

There is a section of New Testament that is referred to during Christmastime, and it can be applied to a marriage perspective as well:

But when he had considered this, behold, an angel of the Lord appeared to him in a dream, saying, "Joseph, son of David, do not be afraid to take Mary as your wife; for the Child who has been conceived in her is of the Holy Spirit (Matthew 1:20).

The angel of the Lord told Joseph not to be afraid to take Mary as his wife. At that point, Joseph and Mary were betrothed but not yet married. When Joseph came to know that Mary was pregnant, he was trying to see how he could get out of that relationship. But the angel of the Lord said to him, "Do not be afraid to take Mary as your wife."

We need to listen to God by saying, "Lord, help me know your will." He will make His message clear through His word, through circumstances, or through people. He will make His will clear if you seek His will. It is important to understand the Lord's will in your life regarding your spouse. The most important thing is to ask whether your partner has accepted Jesus Christ as his or her personal Savior. Trust that God is the One who will bring two people together in marriage, if it is meant to be. We read in Genesis that God himself brought Eve to Adam.

There is another incident in Genesis 24, where Abraham's servant (most likely Eliezer, whose name is mentioned in Genesis 15) went to Abraham's country and found a girl for Isaac. It is very rare that somebody would send a servant to find a girl for his (master's) son? It was the Lord's will that the servant would prayerfully go and find a girl for his master's son Isaac.

Then Isaac brought her into his mother Sarah's tent, and he took Rebekah, and she became his wife, and he loved her; thus Isaac was comforted after his mother's death (Genesis 24:67).

Notice the sequence. Isaac took Rebekah, and she became his wife, and he loved her. The Bible says clearly that Rebekah became Isaac's wife and that he loved her. There is more love *after* marriage than before, because you will likely tend to be more open with your husband or wife than you were in the past. This is when real love develops, when you do not cover up anything. You are not hypocritical; you do not want to impress the other person any more. You are living with that person, and you are not putting on an act anymore. Once he or she becomes your spouse, you start loving that person more.

Biblically speaking, there is love after marriage. May the Lord prepare you for a happy married life so that you will establish a Christian home based on biblical principles!

4. WEDDING AND MARRIAGE

> **What is the difference between marriage and wedding?**
> Marriage is a lifelong relationship between a husband and wife – and it starts on the day of wedding. There is one day you are wedded, and then begins your married life.

There is a difference between "marriage" and "wedding." Marriage is a lifelong relationship between a husband and wife, and it starts on the wedding day. Throughout our days, we have to rejoice in the Lord and praise God by saying, "Lord, it is you who brought us together and made us one flesh." Paul describes in Ephesians 5:23 that Christ is the head of the church, just as the husband is the head of the wife. In verse 32, he mentions that the concept of husband of wife becoming one flesh is a mystery. It is really a mystery how two people from different backgrounds, upbringings, lifestyles—different everything—come together, become one flesh, and start a new life together. How is it possible? It is only because the Lord instituted the marriage and enabled the two persons unite.

After the wedding comes reality. Until then, two unmarried people keep dreaming about how their lives will be, how wonderful it will be for the two of them to be living together after they wed. Practical living experience comes after the wedding day. Those who are married now experience what it takes to come together, having come from different backgrounds, and get to know the things you do not know about the other person. While it is not easy, it is certainly possible, because all things are possible with Christ.

If you are married, you should understand how your home or family ideally should be. If you were not able to set up your home as prescribed in the Bible in the past, do not worry about the past but look ahead to the future and ask God to help you build your Christian home. Past is past. We need to make right decisions for the future based on the Word of God. If we continue pondering the past, we may forget the importance of how we should live now. We should concentrate on how to live as a Christian going forward.

God created man in His own image, in the image of God He created him; male and female, He created them (Genesis 1:27).

Human life began with a marriage. God brought two single people— Adam and Eve, who were created in the image of God—together. One thing we have to understand is that men and women were created in the image of God. Whenever you look at your husband or wife, understand that he or she was created in God's image.

Therefore shall a man leave his father and his mother, and shall cleave unto his wife: and they shall be one flesh (Genesis 2:24

"Leave" does not mean to totally neglect your parents. It means to have allegiance between husband and wife, that when both are married they become one where they pray together and make plans together. However, the relationship with parents continues. Your parents are your parents, and they are your parents forever. You can never say that your relationship with your parents has ended. If you physically leave your parents, the relationship should still be maintained. Many times, the word "leave" is misinterpreted, resulting in ignoring the parents. Once a marriage relationship starts, this new relationship should take precedence, after the relationship with God. It is not that you lose relationships with your parents, brothers, or sisters. God has given you an additional relationship to work with. Earlier, you had three close relationships (with God, parents, and siblings), and now you have a fourth. While the family relationships continue, you spend more time with your spouse and make decisions together prayerfully. That is what the "leaving" and "becoming one flesh" mean.

We can see a whole family for the first time in the Bible in Genesis 2:24. The words "father," "mother," and "wife" are mentioned for the first time. The man here is implied to be the "husband." If the terms father and mother are mentioned, it can be implied that there is a "child" too. Now we have all the relationships of a Christian home right here in verse 24. God brought woman to the man, and they were made one flesh.

Jesus said, "From the beginning of creation, God made them male and female. For this reason, a man shall leave his father and mother, and the two shall become one flesh; so they are no longer two, but one flesh. What therefore God has joined together, let no man separate" (Mark 10:6–9).

Marriage is honorable in all; and the bed undefiled (Hebrews 13:4). It is important to recognize that it is an honorable thing to take part in the experience of marriage.

Go forth, O daughters of Zion, and gaze on King Solomon with the crown, with which his mother has crowned him, on the day of his wedding, and on the day of his gladness of heart (Song of Solomon 3:11).

Notice the phrases "on the day of his wedding" and "gladness of heart." The day of his wedding is the day of his gladness of heart, the day God brings two people together. The day of wedding is a day of gladness. What a joy it is. The joy should not be for the wedding day alone but should continue throughout your married life. Each day becomes a day of rejoicing in the Lord.

Rejoice in the Lord always; again I will say, rejoice! (Philippians 4:4)

Newlyweds

There is a parable mentioned in Luke 14:16–24 where a person was invited for a feast, and he says that he cannot come because he is married.

Another one said, "I have married a wife, and for that reason I cannot come" (Luke 14:20).

What could be the reason for this newly wedded person to reject the invitation? Some quote the following from the Old Testament:

When a man takes a new wife, he shall not go out with the army nor be charged with any duty; he shall be free at home one year and shall give happiness to his wife whom he has taken (Deuteronomy 24:5).

The context in Old Testament is that the man was a soldier and his wife was not. However, as believers in the Lord Jesus Christ, every person is a soldier of Christ. When we are soldiers, we work together. When we work together for the Lord, there is no need to wait for a year or so; let us just work for the Lord. The man in Luke 14 should have said, "I'm married now; let me bring my wife also." Instead, he said he could not come because he is married. One reason could be that they may not have been in agreement to go to a place, and he had to withdraw that invitation. "I got married so I cannot come" is a lame excuse. Marriage relationship should not stop you from working for the Lord. If you are both in Christ and want to make a Christian home, make your home a place where others feel invited and can feel the love and peace flowing through your home.

Partners in Crime?

Every day, the husband and the wife have to live the marriage relationship. They are as two train tracks that are constantly parallel to each other. Do not try to sidetrack but try to keep traveling together. That is when the relationship of marriage comes into perspective. Husbands and wives become partners in everything. Unfortunately, sometimes they end up becoming partners in crime as well. See the lives of Adam and Eve. Adam became a partner in crime with Eve.

When the woman saw that the tree was good for food, and that it was a delight to the eyes, and that the tree was desirable to make one wise, she took from its fruit and ate; and she gave also to her husband with her, and he ate (Genesis 3:6).

We notice that Eve gave also to her husband, Adam, who was with her. Adam became a partner with Eve in the sin of disobedience to God's command. Of course, husband and wife have to be together; however, when it comes to things that are contrary to the Word of God, we should be watchful and not do them. If they continue to do evil things together, both will fall. That is what happened to Adam and Eve. When something is not right according to the Word of God, the other person should correct it. That did not happen in their case, and both slipped into fallen nature. Adam and Eve together committed the sin of disobedience.

Another example of partners in crime is Ananias and Saphira. They are mentioned in Acts chapter 5.

But Peter said, "Ananias, why has Satan filled your heart to lie to the Holy Spirit and to keep back some of the price of the land? While it remained unsold, did it not remain your own? And after it was sold, was it not under your control? Why is it that you have conceived this deed in your heart? You have not lied to men but to God" (Acts 5:3–4).

Ananias did not mention he had kept some money for himself. He lied. And his wife Saphira also did the same thing—she lied. Ananias and Saphira kept a portion for themselves. Maybe they might have thought to save for their future, thinking about their family, settlement, etc. Whatever the reason, they both lied—first Ananias and later Saphira.

Now there elapsed an interval of about three hours, and his wife came in, not knowing what had happened. And Peter responded to her, "Tell me whether you sold the land for such and such a price?" And she said, "Yes, that was the price." Then Peter said to her, "Why is it that you have agreed together to put the Spirit of the Lord to the test? Behold, the feet of those who have buried your husband are at the door, and they will carry you out as well" (Acts 5:7–9).

Ananias and Saphira together committed the sin of lying. Notice the phrase that Peter used: "Agreed together." Of course, husband and wife should agree together, but not to commit any sin. You should not agree to things that are wrong in the sight of God. We should be always watchful as to what things we are agreeing together about. Just question each other: Is it right according to God's Word? If your spouse is doing something wrong, the other person should correct it immediately, and it should be done out of love—do it prayerfully; sit together; show and explain from the Word of God what is right and what is wrong in the sight of God. Do not be like Ananias and Saphira, who together committed the sin of lying and were partners in crime.

Partners in God's Service

An example of good partners is Aquila and Priscilla, who worked together, agreed together, and served God so wonderfully that they brought a person like Apollos to a clear understanding of knowing Jesus Christ as his personal

Savior. Aquila and Priscilla brought Apollos to their "place" (most likely their house), which they kept open for people to come to know God.

Now a Jew named Apollos, an Alexandrian by birth, an eloquent man, came to Ephesus; and he was mighty in the Scriptures. This man had been instructed in the way of the Lord; and being fervent in spirit, he was speaking and teaching accurately the things concerning Jesus, being acquainted only with the baptism of John; and he began to speak out boldly in the synagogue. But when Priscilla and Aquila heard him, they took him aside and explained to him the way of God more accurately (Acts 18:24–26).

Aquila and Priscilla were in agreement for good reasons. God blessed them so much that they were a great blessing to Apollos, who later became a great man of God. Let your married life and your Christian home be a blessing to many others who will be drawn to Christ by seeing the love of Christ through you and in your home.

Relationships

Without relationships, it is hard to survive in this world. You just cannot say, "I want to be all alone; I want to live by myself." God has created us as social beings who desire to interact with others. God is the one who created relationships, and we have to maintain them.

You must have come across the most important words in a relationship:
Six most important words: *I admit I made a mistake*
Five most important words: *You did a great job*
Four most important words: *What do you think?*
Three most important words: *After you, please*
Two most important words: *Thank you*
One most important word: *We*
Least important word: *I*

If there is always just an I in a relationship, then there is no value for that relationship. If you make a mistake, admit it to your spouse. There is nothing wrong in that. If he or she did something good and praiseworthy, learn to attribute good words and thanks to your spouse. If you are making any important decisions, consult with each other and ask, "What do you think?" and seek each other's suggestions. Husbands should not think, *I am the head of the house and I will make decisions myself*, and wives should not think, *My husband is poor at handling matters, so let me just handle myself and I don't need his consent.* Always consult with each other on any purchase, any choice to go somewhere, or when making any important decision. Also, learn to give your spouse a chance; be patient. This enables the couple to become stronger in their relationship with each other, which leads us to what a couple means in the next chapter.

5. COUPLE

A nd the two shall become one flesh; so they are no longer two, but one flesh (Mark 10:8).

When two people are married, they are called a married couple. It is important for married people to understand what it means to be a couple.

Acronym of C-O-U-P-L-E

C: Closeness/Cherishing
For this reason, a man shall leave his father and his mother, and be joined to his wife; and they shall become one flesh. (Genesis 2:24)
So husbands ought also to love their own wives as their own bodies. He who loves his own wife loves himself; for no one ever hated his own flesh, but nourishes and cherishes it, just as Christ also does the church (Ephesians 5:28-29)

O: Openness
My beloved spoke and said to me, "Arise, my darling, my beautiful one, come with me. (Song of Solomon 2:10)

U: Understanding
You husbands in the same way live with your wives in an understanding way, as with someone weaker, since she is a woman; and show her honor as a fellow heir of the grace of life, so that your prayers will not be hindered. (1 Peter 3:7)

P: Peacemaking
Be angry, and yet do not sin; do not let the sun go down on your anger. (Ephesians 4:26)

L: Love/Loyal
Love is patient, love is kind and is not jealous; love does not brag and is not arrogant. (1 Corinthians 13:4)
Husband of one wife (Titus 1:6)

E: Encouraging/Esteeming
But encourage one another day after day, as long as it is still called "Today," so that none of you will be hardened by the deceitfulness of sin. (Hebrews 3:13)
In lowliness of mind let each esteem other better than themselves. (Philippians 2:3)

Closeness

For this reason, a man shall leave his father and his mother, and be joined to his wife; and they shall become one flesh (Genesis 2:24).

Husbands and wives draw closer to each other after marriage. The closer you are, the stronger your relationship. Bonding happens when you bring two things together. You might have studied about chemical bonding or amalgamation, which is the process of combining or uniting multiple entities into one. Only when two elements are brought together, a reaction happens. You should be so close to each other that nothing or no one should come between you. Share with each other what happened throughout the day. Keep communicating with each other, be it small or large things. By staying close to each other, you will know what your spouse likes or dislikes, what kinds of things he or she might do and not do, and you will learn to take good care of each other. Your example should lead the younger couples to grow closer to each other.

Cherishing

So husbands ought also to love their own wives as their own bodies. He who loves his own wife loves himself; for no one ever hated his own flesh, but nourishes and cherishes it, just as Christ also does the church, because we are members of His body (Ephesians 5:28–30).

The two rhyming words mentioned above are "nourish" and "cherish". The original Greek word for "cherish" is *"thalpo,"* meaning "to keep warm," or "to cherish with tender love," or "to foster with tender care." Keeping warm would definitely require the couple involved to stay or be close together. Just as Christ cherished the church, the couple needs to cherish one another by showing tender loving care. You need to take care of your spouse or family in various situations—physically, emotionally, and spiritually. The more you draw nearer to God and His Word, the more you draw nearer to each other in fellowship. Cherish the moments that you spend together by giving thanks to God for each other.

Openness

My beloved responded and said to me, "Arise, my darling, my beautiful one, and come along" (Song of Solomon 2:10).

You may wonder how 'closeness' and 'openness' can go hand in hand. Closeness is physical closeness. Openness is being open-minded. You should try to open up to your wife or husband. Try to share whatever is going on in your mind. It does not matter whether you are wrong; your spouse may correct you. Do not try to cover things up or be secretive. If you start maintaining secrets, you will start lying, and your relationship will be affected. Openness happens when you talk to—communicate with—each other. Spend time with each other, and respond to one another. When your husband or wife talks to you, don't just keep quiet, respond by saying whether you agree or disagree, or pray about it, or try to discover the Lord's will about it. Then you can both come to one peaceful understanding of what you plan to do.

You should speak out and communicate well. If you do not talk to each other, and if you are not open to each other's thoughts and ideas, many misunderstandings creep up. Lot of misunderstandings arises because of lack of communication or miscommunication. Even in secular projects or work places, communication is given much importance, because many devastating things happen when there is a gap in communication. So much importance should be given to communication in your family life and daily living! Do not worry if you do not have a topic to open up with. Song of Solomon 2:10–13 mentions seasons, flowers, birds, fruits, etc. as topics. You can talk about seasons, weather conditions, and important decisions in your home. Be open and try to relate as much as possible with your spouse.

Understanding

You husbands in the same way live with your wives in an understanding way, as with someone weaker, since she is a woman; and show her honor as a fellow heir of the grace of life, so that your prayers will not be hindered (1 Peter 3:7).

How can you live in an understanding way? The fear of the Lord is the beginning of wisdom or understanding. Here, Peter mentions woman as the weaker vessel. That is fine, because God has created woman the way she is. If you have two vessels—copper and porcelain—the porcelain vessel has to be handled carefully. The same is the case with women, who are fashioned by God. We have to understand each other; personalities will differ. Some may be emotional, and some may appear strong but are sensitive at heart. Just be watchful of the personality of your spouse, and understand your spouse and handle matters accordingly. Ask the Lord to give you understanding and wisdom to deal with the situations you are going through, and live in an understanding way.

Peacemaking

Be angry, and yet do not sin; do not let the sun go down on your anger (Ephesians 4:26).

Try to come to a peaceful conclusion when you are trying to decide something. Try to resolve the issues prayerfully even before the sun sets. Try to go to sleep peacefully. If you carry your anger to the next day, the next day will also be badly affected. If you do not agree about something, you should pray together and ask the Lord to bring you both to a common ground. The Lord can change you or your spouse, or the Lord can change the thought itself, and both of you might agree for a different reason. Maintaining peace is important for Christian homes. And the peace of God, which passeth all understanding, shall keep your hearts and minds through Christ Jesus (Philippians 4:7 KJV). Jesus is the prince of peace (Isaiah 9:6). When we have such a God who is peace and gives us peace, why do not we apply it in our homes?

Christian homes should have peace flowing through them. For that, you have to come to your knees when there are unresolved issues in your family. Family prayers are important for Christian homes. The time of family prayer will bring the family members to one level. You should not be concerned over trivial things such as whether you should have family prayer before or after dinner, and such things as this. The concern should be whether you are having family prayers in a manner that bring the family members closer to God and each other. You should not just read a verse, pray, and go to sleep. If you participate in family prayer, study the word of God as a family, taking turns so that everyone can join in. Spend time with the Lord to know His will regarding any major decisions, and your spouse or other family members will learn from you if they don't know how to know God's will.

Love

Love is patient, love is kind and is not jealous; love does not brag and is not arrogant, does not act unbecomingly; it does not seek its own, is not provoked, does not take into account a wrong suffered, does not rejoice in unrighteousness, but rejoices with the truth; bears all things, believes all things, hopes all things, endures all things. Love never fails (1 Corinthians 13:4–8).

We have already seen from the word of God that husbands should love their wives, and wives should love their husbands. A marriage relationship should have love as a foundation. Love covers many things. If you love your spouse, you can overcome many weaknesses and live together under the same roof.

Loyalty

Husband of one wife (Titus 1:6).

The wedding vows say, "I will be loyal to my husband" or "I will be loyal to my wife." It means he or she, and nobody else, is preeminent for the rest of our lives together. Many people are loyal to the brands they buy. Some buy the same make of a vehicle and stay loyal to it. When you care so much about nonliving things, imagine how much loyalty you should show toward your wife or husband, whom you have married and promised to take care of for the rest of your life. You should be able to tell your spouse "I need your cooperation for now and always."

Encouraging

But encourage one another day after day, as long as it is still called "Today," so that none of you will be hardened by the deceitfulness of sin (Hebrews 3:13).

Encourage one another. Do not discourage or demean him or her. If you keep blaming your spouse, he or she will be discouraged. Even in difficult situations, such as loss of job or financial problem or any kind of mistakes that were made, try to deal with a cool mind, and handle together the steps you need to take next. Depend on the Lord, and He will guide you.

Encourage each other out of love. Assure your spouse that it is okay if the food was not cooked properly, or if the job interview did not go well. Encourage by saying he or she can do better next time. If you start shouting at each other, you will demean the other person and lose your testimony. Instead, seek God's help in any kind of situation, and handle with love. Hebrews 3:13 says, "Day after day." Whom do you meet on a daily basis?

You do not meet your church members daily. This verse can be aptly applied to the person closest to you—your husband or your wife.

Esteeming

Let nothing be done through strife or vainglory; but in lowliness of mind let each esteem other better than themselves. (Philippians 2:3).

Esteem others better than yourself. Esteem your husband or wife better than yourself. Do not always think that you alone can make the best decision and your spouse cannot. Do not think that you alone are good at something and your spouse is not. Just understand that he or she is better at some things and let that person handle those things. You might be weak in some areas while your spouse may excel in them, and vice versa. God brought you together to complement each other. Just be thankful to the Lord that your spouse is strong when you are weak. Do not put any restrictions around you by saying that he or she is trying to barge in on your comfort zone or arena. However, be happy he or she can share your weaknesses and strengths and share all your joys and difficulties. If you start considering your spouse may be better than you at certain things, you may discover your spouse's many hidden skills and talents. In addition, together use your skills, talents, and time for the Lord's glory and the extension of His kingdom, which will have eternal value.

6. HUSBAND AND WIFE

Let us look into what it takes for a husband and wife to build a Christian home.

The wise woman builds her house, but the foolish tears it down with her own hands. He who walks in his uprightness fears the LORD, but he who is devious in his ways despises Him (Proverbs 14:1–2).

"The wise woman builds her house"—wisdom is necessary when building a house. Woman is mentioned specifically here because she is also responsible in the building of a house. The book of proverbs concentrates on the importance of having wisdom. Verse 1 speaks of woman, and verse 2 speaks of man. These two verses are important because together, a man (husband) and a woman (wife) set up a home.

When husband and wife come together as a family, God should give you the wisdom to setup your home and start a family life together. You must have the uprightness of heart and fear of Lord God, who will give you wisdom and guide you in building your home. Fear of the Lord is important. Do not do as you please but seek what pleases God. The three qualities that are mentioned in Proverbs 14:1–2 are wisdom, uprightness of heart, and fear of the Lord. These are important in building a Christian home. If you try to build something without these three qualities, you will not have a strong foundation.

Unless the Lord builds the house, they labor in vain that build it (Psalm 127:1).

If you do not seek the Lord's guidance, then you are building your house in vain. In Psalm 127, we see that the Lord builds the house, while in Proverbs 14 we see the husband and wife are responsible for building the house. God is the chief architect, and we are the builders. He directs us. He gives us the wisdom and appropriate guidance to build our homes in the light of His Word.

Let us examine the responsibilities of husband and wife. Word of God is like an instruction manual. If you are not yet married, remember these responsibilities for your future. There are many books in the market that guide husbands and wives to lead happy lives. However, the most important book to read for building up a Christian home is the Bible. The Bible can never be substituted for any other book. Even if you read other books, always check whether the principle is in accordance with the Word of God. The Bible should be the basis and a reference point.

HUSBAND	WIFE
1. Trust The heart of her husband trusts in her. (Proverbs 31:11)	**1. Fear God** A woman who fears the LORD, she shall be praised. (Proverbs 31:30)
2. Praise/Encouragement Her husband also, and he praises her. (Proverbs 31:28)	**2. Excellent/Virtuous** An excellent wife is the crown of her husband (Proverbs 12:4) Who can find a virtuous woman? for her price is far above rubies. (Proverbs 31:10)
3. Love So husbands ought also to love their own wives as their own bodies. He who loves his own wife loves himself. (Ephesians 5:28)	**3. Trustworthiness** The heart of her husband trusts in her, and he will have no lack of gain. (Proverbs 31:11)
4. Honor Show her honor as a fellow heir of the grace of life. (1 Peter 3:7)	**4. Do good and not evil** She does him good and not evil all the days of her life. (Proverbs 31:12)
5. Provide But if anyone does not provide for his own, and especially for those of his household, he has denied the faith and is worse than an unbeliever. (1 Timothy 5:8)	**5. Give importance** Her husband is known in the gates, when he sits among the elders of the land. (Proverbs 31:23)

First, let us see from the Word of God how a husband is responsible for building a Christian home.

Responsibilities of the Husband

1. Trust

The heart of her husband trusts in her (Proverbs 31:11).

Proverbs 31 talks mostly about woman. You may wonder where a husband comes into the picture. Verse 11 says that the heart of her *husband* trusts in her. It is not just saying with words that you trust her, your heart should trust her as well. Trusting your wife is important. You should have the trust relationship to build a home. If you do not trust your wife, you do not have the foundation for a good relationship. If you do not trust your wife, you tend to go to somebody else to share your concerns, which is not good for your relationship. If you do not trust each other, there will be a wall of separation between you. Spend time with each other and with God together so that he will build up your trust in Him, as well between each other.

2. Praise/Encouragement

Her husband also, and he praises her (Proverbs 31:28).

Her husband praises her. It is not a bad thing to say words of praise to your wife. Your ego does not get affected. Instead, your wife will like you more, and she will get encouraged. It is good to appreciate your wife. Tell her she did a good job. If you do not praise your wife and others do, she will not be happy with you either. A husband's words of praise or encouragement give contentment and happiness to his wife. Be genuine and say it in a heartfelt way, rather than just saying the words without meaning them.

3. Love

So husbands ought also to love their own wives as their own bodies. He who loves his own wife loves himself (Ephesians 5:28).

Love your wife. Trust and love are strong pillars for a healthy marriage relationship. Husbands ought to love their wives. You have to love your wife—it is a commandment, and there is no alternative. "Love your neighbor as yourself" (Matthew 22:39) is a generic statement, while "love your wife as yourself" (Ephesians 5:33) is a specific statement. The

Bible is consistent. When the word of God says, "Love your neighbor as yourself," why should you not apply it in your own home? Love your wife as yourself.

Nevertheless, each individual among you also is to love his own wife even as himself, and the wife must see to it that she respects her husband (Ephesians 5:33).

Yet you say, "For what reason?" Because the LORD has been a witness between you and the wife of your youth, against whom you have dealt treacherously, though she is your companion and your wife by covenant. But not one has done so who has a remnant of the Spirit And what did that one do while he was seeking a godly offspring? Take heed then to your spirit, and let no one deal treacherously against the wife of your youth (Malachi 2:14–15).

Here, God is talking about His relationship with people, comparing it to the relationship between husband and wife. Your wife is your companion. You made a covenant with her and promises to each other. Love and be faithful to your wife. The same things apply to wives, to love their husbands and be faithful to them.

4. Honor

Show her honor as a fellow heir of the grace of life (1 Peter 3:7).

The verse says, "Show her honor." Many husbands do not like the idea of honoring their wives. It impacts their chauvinism or ego. If you want to follow God's word, honor your wife. She is your wife, and she deserves honor. She is a fellow heir of the grace of life. She is also a fellow child in the kingdom of God. God made us His children because of His grace. When the Bible says that marriage is honorable above all, such honor should be reflected in relationship with your spouse.

5. Provide

But if anyone does not provide for his own, and especially for those of his household, he has denied the faith and is worse than an unbeliever (1 Timothy 5:8).

Husbands have the primary responsibility to provide for the needs of the house. Sometimes, you care for the needs of other people and neglect your own family. If the husband does not provide for his wife and family, the family members would be concerned. If the husband is not concerned about his family's wellbeing, then coordination and cooperation between husband and wife will be lost. If you do not consult your wife and ask her what she thinks, a gap will form between you. The husband has to provide for the physical and spiritual needs and the security of the family. He should take the responsibility for physical as well as spiritual protection. He has to provide for the needs of the household, as he is the head of the family. He should protect the family from all kind of dangers, both physically and spiritually. He has to pacify the family members emotionally. In 1 Timothy 5:8, it says if he does not provide for his own, and especially for those of his household, he has denied the faith and is worse than an unbeliever. How terrible that would be. When God created us as men, and specifically as husbands, He entrusted us with many responsibilities, and we need to take care of the physical, spiritual, financial, and emotional needs of the family.

Let us now examine the responsibilities of a wife in building up a Christian home.

Wife

1. God-fearing

A woman who fears the LORD, she shall be praised (Proverbs 31:30).

We have seen earlier (Proverbs 14:2) that a man should be upright and fear the Lord. Here in Proverbs 31:30, we see that a woman should be God fearing, and she shall be praised. If husband and wife are God fearing, what a wonderful home that will be. They will automatically teach their children to fear the Lord. Their home will be a great example of a Christian home.

2. Excellent/Virtuous

An excellent wife is the crown of her husband. An excellent wife, who can find? For her worth is far above jewels (Proverbs 12:4; 31:10).

If a husband is the head of the family, then his wife should be like a crown on that head, because an excellent wife is the "crown" of her husband. The crown is seen, and it should make the husband look good on the outside. A tiara or crown is placed on the head and signifies honor. A bride puts on a crown or a tiara, which gives her honor and beauty. A king or a queen dons a crown to show his or her honor or position.

There is a well-known truism, "Behind a man's success is a woman." The Word of God says, "An excellent wife is the crown of her husband." There is no superlative to the word "excellent." Maybe the word "excellent" has higher significance than the word "best." In other translations, it means "virtuous." Wives have to understand the importance of being "crowns" to their husbands and should strive to be virtuous and excellent.

3. Trustworthiness

The heart of her husband trusts in her, and he will have no lack of gain (Proverbs 31:11).

A husband will trust his wife only when she's trustworthy. You have to cling to the promises you made to each other. The vows or promises are not just for the wedding day but for the whole of your lives together. After you are married, the husband should be the wife's priority, after God. You should build trust between each other to share all things. If your husband learns of any personal matter from others and not from you, this may make him lose trust in you, and vice versa. Therefore, it is better to share things with your husband and be trustworthy. You should be able to keep up that trust.

4. Do Good and Not Evil

She does him good and not evil all the days of her life (Proverbs 31:12).

"All the days of her life" means in sickness or in health, or in adversity or prosperity. In all situations, a wife should do good and not evil. Husband and wife should stick with each other through all kinds of situations, including difficulties. You may go through emotional or financial difficulties or through difficulties relating to your spouse's family; whatever tough situation you are going through, just perform acts of good and not evil. Husband and wife should be together, stay strong, and do good and not evil deeds. When the wife does well, her family praises her. The husband and children are praising her because she fears God, does good deeds, and is praiseworthy.

Her children rise up and bless her; Her husband also, and he praises her, saying: Many daughters have done nobly, But you excel them all (Proverbs 31:28–29).

5. Give Importance to Your Husband

Her husband is known in the gates, when he sits among the elders of the land (Proverbs 31:23).

The wife should make sure her husband is given priority over other things or relationships; she should support him and give respect to him. She should prove herself to be a "crown" of her husband. Then the husband will have a good name. This implies the relationship between the husband and wife is an exemplary one. Then the husband is well known outside the home. That is a testimony for others to see.

When somebody visits you, he or she should be able to say that there is peace in your house. You should live as examples for others to follow.

Examine Yourself

- Is your home based on love and trust?

- Are you faithful toward each other?

- Are you patient toward each other?

- Do you give importance to each other?

All the above responsibilities of husband and wife have to be conducted mutually, out of love and trust toward each other, which are important pillars toward a solid foundation for a healthy relationship. There are two houses mentioned in the Bible: a house built upon a rock and a house built upon sand. The house built upon a rock will stay firm even when there are storms, unlike the house built upon the sand, which is destroyed by winds. Your house should be strong, like the house built upon a rock, and Jesus Christ should be the rock, the center, the foundation and priority of your home. Love God and trust in Him. As you love your spouse, continue to trust in each other and keep open communication between both of you. It enables vertical and horizontal relationships to remain strong and unshaken.

Let love and faithfulness never leave you; bind them around your neck, write them on the tablet of your heart (Proverbs 3:3).

If a husband and wife never let love and faithfulness leave them, there will never be a chance for the enemy to cause misunderstanding between them.

We need to build our homes seeking the Lord's wisdom and guidance. God will give you grace and wisdom to love your spouse unconditionally and be able to trust in that person. As mentioned in Ephesians 5:22 and 5:25, husbands have to love their wives, and wives have to submit to their husbands, and the relationship between them should signify the relationship between Christ and the church. That is how Christian homes are built up. Some people say they can love but not submit. We have to obey the word of God fully. If God has given us those instructions, we have to follow them. God is the master builder; He is the architect. It is God who makes foundations for our houses, and we just need to follow Him. The Bible tells wives to submit to their husbands as you do unto the Lord. Husbands, love your wives as Christ has loved you. Always remember how the husband and wife relationship is linked to our relationship with Christ. Our utmost priority should be God always. Christ is the head of the church and the husband is the head of the wife (Ephesians 5:23).

7. Unbelieving Spouse

It is possible that a husband or wife may not be a believer in Lord Jesus Christ. The Word of God clearly guides us to build our homes in a godly way. Both 1 Corinthians 7 and 1 Peter 3 mention the believer and unbeliever spouses. They cannot be yoked together. If you are not married, be very careful who you choose. But, if you are married, then the believer's life should hopefully affect the unbelieving spouse, and through prayer, the Lord would work in the heart of the unbelieving spouse. The word "sanctified" is used in 1 Corinthians 7:14, that the unbelieving husband is sanctified through his wife, and the unbelieving wife is sanctified through her believing husband.

For the unbelieving husband is sanctified through his wife, and the unbelieving wife is sanctified through her believing husband, for otherwise your children are unclean, but now they are holy. For how do you know, O wife, whether you will save your husband? Or how do you know, O husband, whether you will save your wife? (1 Corinthians 7:14, 16).

In the same way, you wives, be submissive to your own husbands so that even if any of them are disobedient to the word, they may be won without a word by the behavior of their wives, as they observe your chaste and respectful behavior (1 Peter 3:1–2).

It is not by your words that you can change your spouse or bring him or her to Christ, but by your behavior and in the way you are submissive and loving. If you are a wife of an unbelieving husband, your husband will slowly start changing when he realizes you love him in spite of his reactions toward you. He will realize there is something unique in his wife, and that will enable him to change. If you are a husband of an unbelieving wife, be patient towards her and keep praying, and she will know God's love through you.

There should be a difference between a believer and an unbeliever. Otherwise, unbelievers will mock you, saying, "What difference is there between you and me? You do all the things I do. The only difference is, you go to church, and I don't." If that is the case, you are not bringing glory to God, and you are not bringing sanctification to the other person. Remember, you are separated, chosen, and called out, people. Moreover, you have to show that difference through your words, actions, thoughts, and love. Your spouse should recognize that the difference in you is because of Christ in you. It may take time for your spouse to change—maybe a year, maybe two years, maybe ten or even more than that. You just need to pray with a lot of zeal and hope, and the Lord will answer your prayers and do wonders in His own time. You have the spiritual responsibility to love, witness, and attract him or her to the Savior.

If your spouse is an unbeliever, your children will be affected by that, as we have seen mentioned in 1 Corinthians chapter 7. In such a case, when you have an unbelieving spouse, you have additional responsibility of bringing up your children in a godly way. A great example is Eunice, the mother of Timothy. Her husband was Greek, not a Jew and not a Christian (Acts 16:1). She led the life of a godly wife by bearing the double burden of an unequal yoke (2 Corinthians 6:14). She had more responsibility toward her son to bring him up in the Lord.

And that from childhood you have known the sacred writings which are able to give you the wisdom that leads to salvation through faith which is in Christ Jesus. (2 Timothy 3:15).

Eunice proved to be a faithful mother in being both spiritual mother and father to Timothy. See the phrase "from infancy" in verse 15. The upbringing could be seen when Timothy became an evangelist (2 Timothy 4:5). Eunice might have greatly rejoiced.

Let your father and your mother be glad, and let her rejoice who gave birth to you (Proverbs 23:25).

8. IN-LAWS

Let us look at how you should maintain relationships with your in-laws. Some in-laws are mentioned in the Bible, and we can learn through those relationships.

Daughter- and Mother-in-law

A great example of an exemplary daughter- and mother-in-law relationship is Ruth and Naomi. Ruth lived with mother-in-law Naomi. The main point here is that they were working out their relationship and made great sacrifices for one another.

So she stayed close by the maids of Boaz in order to glean until the end of the barley harvest and the wheat harvest. And she lived with her mother-in-law (Ruth 2:23).

Then Naomi her mother-in-law said to her, "My daughter, shall I not seek security for you, that it may be well with you?" (Ruth 3:1)

Naomi was concerned for Ruth. It is important, because mother-in-law is also a mother. Never say your mother-in-law can never be like a mother to you, or that your daughter-in-law can never be like a daughter to you. In Ruth 3:1, Naomi called Ruth her daughter. We have to try to maintain such a relationship with our in-laws as well.

Son- and Mother-in-law

And immediately after they came out of the synagogue, they came into the house of Simon and Andrew, with James and John. Now Simon's mother-in-law was lying sick with a fever; and immediately they spoke to Jesus about her (Mark 1:29–30).

Mark 1 gives another example of the in-law relationship, this time between son- and mother-in-law. Here, Simon's mother-in-law fell sick. They prayed for her; they talked to Jesus about her. At that time, they physically went to Jesus on her behalf.

At this time, we need to spend time in prayer. Pray for your mother-in-law or father-in-law if is she or he is physically or spiritually sick. Spend time in prayer if she or he is going through difficulties. You can only pray when you are concerned for your in-laws. Have concern toward them, and show your concern. Notice in the passage that James, John, and Jesus came along with others. They were having fellowship and prayed for Simon's sick mother-in-law . They spoke to Jesus, and Jesus healed her. Speak to Jesus in today's world through prayer. We need to pray for our in-laws.

Son- and Father-in-law

Exodus 18 records a conversation between a son-in-law and father-in-law, Moses and Jethro.

Moses's father-in-law said to him, "The thing that you are doing is not good. You will surely wear out, both yourself and these people who are with you, for the task is too heavy for you; you cannot do it alone.... Furthermore, you shall select out of all the people able men who fear God, men of truth, those who hate dishonest gain; and you shall place these over them as leaders of thousands, of hundreds, of fifties and of tens." So Moses listened to his father-in-law and did all that he had said (Exodus 18:17–18, 21, 24).

Imagine a father-in-law telling his son-in-law that whatever the son-in-law is doing is not good. The son-in-law would hesitate to listen to the next word the father-in-law speaks because the son-in-law might get angry. God used Jethro to guide Moses because Moses was acting as prophet and judge and was handling many things. Jethro advised Moses to delegate the responsibilities to able men and to those who fear God. If you are going to select someone for the work of the Lord, they should be able to do the work, and they should be God fearing. They should be men of truth and not hypocrites. They should hate dishonest gain; they should not try to get profit from doing God's work. Jethro gave that advice to Moses, and Moses listened. It is okay to listen to your in-laws. God can use different people to guide you. Jethro gave Moses godly advice. If somebody gives you godly advice, including your father-in-law, consider the advice.

However, be watchful of certain types of in-laws. Consider the case of Jacob and his father-in-law, Laban (Genesis 29). Laban was not a trustworthy father-in-law. He deceived Jacob by letting him serve for a total of fourteen years to ultimately marry Rachel. Yet, out of his love towards Rachel, Jacob patiently served his father-in-law. Towards the later part of his life, Laban told Jacob, "If now it pleases you, stay with me; I have divined that the LORD has blessed me on your account" (Genesis 30:27).

Relationship with in-laws is critical in building a godly home. Remember they are your spouse's parents, as well as your children's grandparents. They are part of your family, where love and honor needs to be expressed with each other. Even though there may be challenges in the relationship, if you take the responsibility of showing love and honor, the relationship will get stronger. We need to pray for our in-laws and relate to them just as we relate to our parents, and maintain the relationship for the glory of God.

9. Parents

It is a great mystery how two people from different backgrounds become "one." It is mentioned in the Bible; Paul calls it a mystery. A Christian home is made up of two people becoming "one", and then that "one" gets multiplied to many. For those who are married and do not yet have children, or those not yet married, this section will be good preparation for your blessed future.

Before Conceiving

What is your responsibility before you have children? The answer is to pray.

Isaac prayed to the LORD on behalf of his wife, because she was barren; and the LORD answered him and Rebekah his wife conceived (Genesis 25:21).

Isaac prayed to the Lord before his wife conceived. Everything should start with prayer. Pray for your child before the child is conceived in the mother's womb. Isaac prayed to the Lord on behalf of his wife, and the Lord answered him. Before Isaac married Rebecca, when Rebecca was coming to meet Isaac, Isaac was praying (Genesis 24:63). Now Isaac prayed to the Lord, and Rebecca conceived.

Benjamin Mittapalli

After Conceiving

Then Manoah entreated the LORD and said, "O Lord, please let the man of God whom You have sent come to us again that he may teach us what to do for the boy who is to be born" (Judges 13:8).

In this passage, Manoah (father of Samson) came to know his wife is pregnant, and he is praying to the Lord. What a wonderful prayer that is, toward a child yet-to-be born. A Christian mom-to-be or dad-to-be should pray and learn from God's Word how to bring up the child in the fear and favor of God.

After the Birth

Now that a child has been born into the Christian home, what is the responsibility of the parents? Both parents have to be united and prayerful in whatever decisions they will make regarding the child. When naming the child, many parents will be in a dilemma, unable to choose one or the other, and in such cases they should just wait on the Lord for complete peace in choosing a name.

And it happened that on the eighth day they came to circumcise the child, and they were going to call him Zacharias, after his father. But his mother answered and said, "No indeed; but he shall be called John." And they said to her, "There is no one among your relatives who is called by that name." And they made signs to his father, as to what he wanted him called. And he asked for a tablet and wrote as follows, "His name is John." And they were all astonished. And at once his mouth was opened and his tongue loosed, and he began to speak in praise of God (Luke 1:59–64).

Here we see the unity of parents-to-be. When the Lord spoke to Zacharias, he was made to keep quiet until the baby was born. However, Zecharias did not stop communicating with his wife. He could not open his mouth, but he wrote, "His name is John." It is important for husband and wife to be united and to do so prayerfully, even while choosing a name for their child.

PARENTS

1. Teach your children

These words, which I am commanding you today, shall be on your heart. You shall teach them diligently to your sons and shall talk of them when you sit in your house and when you walk by the way and when you lie down and when you rise up. (Deuteronomy 6:6-7)

2. Train your children

Train up a child in the way he should go, even when he is old he will not depart from it. (Proverbs 22:6)

3. Bring them up in discipline

Fathers, do not provoke your children to anger, but bring them up in the discipline and instruction of the Lord. (Ephesians 6:4)

4. Set an example

Follow God's example, therefore, as dearly loved children. (Ephesians 5:1)

5. Share the importance of salvation

They said, "Believe in the Lord Jesus, and you will be saved, you and your household." (Acts 16:31)

Responsibilities of a Parent

1. Teach Your Children

These words, which I am commanding you today, shall be on your heart. You shall teach them diligently to your sons and shall talk of them when you sit in your house and when you walk by the way and when you lie down and when you rise up (Deuteronomy 6: 6–7).

Do not think that only Sunday-school teachers or other outsiders should teach your children. It is the parents' duty to teach their children about God. Children may be taught Bible lessons by their teachers, but the basic foundation should be laid at home. It is the responsibility of the parents to impart the Word of God to your children. Do not procrastinate to teach godly things to your child, thinking he may not understand now. A child's character develops from a young age, so it is important to bring him or her up from birth in the discipline and instruction of the Lord.

2. Train Your Children

Train up a child in the way he should go, even when he is old he will not depart from it (Proverbs 22:6).

This verse mentions training children, while Deuteronomy 6:6 mentions teaching children. the difference between teaching and training is that - teaching is theoretical, while training is practical. You should not only teach but also be practical in showing your children how to apply the teachings too. Therefore, training helps build up the child practically so the child will learn by watching the parents, and this will have more impact on the child.

3. Bring Them Up in Discipline

Fathers, do not provoke your children to anger, but bring them up in the discipline and instruction of the Lord (Ephesians 6:4).

Paul uses the phrase "bring them up." Children are also apt to get angry, so try to prevent them from getting angry, but bringing them up in the discipline and instruction of the Lord. Discipline is important, and it can be imparted in a loving manner. A sentence can be told in two different ways: either in a harsh way or in a calm way that the child can understand. We should know how to talk to our children and develop close relationships with them so they will confide in us, share things with us, and easily reach us whenever they need to.

4. Set an Example

Therefore be imitators of God, as beloved children (Ephesians 5:1).

Children will be greatly impacted when they see their mom and dad living as believing parents. Those of us, who witnessed believing parents walking in the way of the Lord, know what a blessing that is. Be thankful to God and your parents for that wonderful blessing. In addition, those of us who did not have believing parents know what a feeling that is, and we should understand the importance of Christian upbringing.

We have to be an example to our kids in what we say, what we do, what we watch, and what we hear. We should not just be telling our kids to pray, but showing them that we pray regularly and encourage them to pray. Your children will be observing your prayer life; they check if your daily living matches what you preach. Your children should know that God is your priority, and they should see that in your life.

If any family related decision has to be made, the parents should first come to a common ground and then share the decision with the children. Otherwise, if one parent says yes and the other says no, it amounts to confusion and misunderstanding. If husband and wife keep shouting at and fighting with each other, the children will be negatively affected by their bad example. When the children later build their own families, they will look back at how their parents behaved. They should have good memories of parents who maintained good relationship with each other and the children.

You may think you are free to do anything in your home and your neighbors will not know it. Many times you forget about your children who live right in your house and are affected by all your doings. Do not be hypocritical. If you fear God and want to follow Jesus, who is a great example for all of us, your personality and temperament should reflect that you are a Christian. Behave the same way in front or back of others.

A daughter will look up to her mother, who sets a good example in the way she dresses, cooks, cleans, and sets up a Christian home. A son will want a wife who has the same qualities as his mother, who set a good example of being a wife and mother. A son will look up to his father, who set a good example in being responsible, reachable, attending to his family's needs, and setting up a Christian home. A daughter will want a husband who has the qualities as her father, who set a good example as a husband and father.

5. Share the Importance of Salvation

They said, "Believe in the Lord Jesus, and you will be saved, you and your household" (Acts 16:31).

When your children are growing up, keep sharing the importance of salvation—what it means and how one can be saved. It is not in our hands but in God's will when they will accept Jesus Christ as their personal Savior. We have to let them know how important salvation and eternal life are. Never try to force the kids to accept Christ, to make a decision immediately, or to be baptized immediately. Many children keep complaining at a later point in time that they were forced to take baptism.

The Holy Spirit of God should convince them about their stand for Christ, and that is when they will firmly stand for the Lord, and not shake. If they reject the gospel, do not get angry with them, but keep praying for them, and the Lord will do wonders in His own time.

I have no greater joy than to hear that my children are walking in the truth (3 John 1:4).

It is such a joy to see our children saved and having the fear of the Lord. That should be each and every Christian parent's joy, prayer, and testimony. Once the children are saved, God will take care of them, whatever position they might be in. God will never forsake His children. Our duty as parents is to pray for our children fervently. Job 1:5 mentions that Job, a great man of God, continuously prayed for his children and offered burnt sacrifices, thinking his children might have done any mistakes.

Children are a gift of the LORD. The fruit of the womb is a reward (Psalm 127:3). Prayerful parents have a great impact on their children. It depends on how much foundation is being laid by parents, and how much time is being spent instilling the fear of the Lord in the children. It is important for godly parents to bring up godly children. More than children, consider them gifts and rewards from the Lord.

6. Be stewards of God's gift

Parents are like stewards of God to raise their children. This means God is going to take an account of how we are bringing up the children He has given us. When God gives us gifts in the form of children, He gives us additional responsibilities as well. If you have a baby, you will have sleepless nights, no proper food, 24/7 cleaning to do (e.g., disinfecting the baby's sleeping area, making sure the house is germ free), continuous monitoring of the baby, etc., and everything comes with the package. When you become a parent, your responsibilities increase. Your life was so different when you did not have kids. You were just two people, and now you have a third person who is the product of you both. Now your life will revolve around your child. With few more additions, your responsibilities increase even more. What a joy it will be to see physical growth in your children, and what a greater joy it is to see the children growing up in the Lord right from childhood.

God expects us to take care of our children and be accountable to Him for the way we bring them up and how we deal with them. When Pharaoh's daughter found the baby Moses in the basket in river Nile, she owned the baby and gave the baby to Moses's own mother, Jochebed, telling her to feed him and take care of him (see Exodus 2:9). That is a metaphor for God giving us children and asking us to take care of them.

When Israel saw the sons of Joseph, he asked, "Who are these?" "They are the sons God has given me here," Joseph said to his father. Then Israel said, "Bring them to me so I may bless them." Joseph said that his sons were given by God. And Jacob blessed Joseph's sons Genesis 48:8–9).

When Joseph introduced his children to Jacob, he mentioned them as God's gifts to him. You should be able to bless your children—not just in the literal way, as in when they sneeze and you say, "God bless you". It is important that the parents not only to encourage and exhort the children but also bless them.

7. Let Children be Signs and Wonders

Behold, I and the children whom the LORD has given me are for signs and wonders in Israel from the LORD of hosts, who dwells on Mount Zion (Isaiah 8:18).

Our children are like signs and wonders. Children should be like signs, showing Jesus to others and showing the way, proclaiming Jesus is the way, the truth, and the life. Children should be like wonders as well, and it will be wonderful to see the kids have the fear of the Lord, obey parents and elders, study well, and be great examples for others.

Men of Israel, listen to these words: Jesus the Nazarene, a man attested to you by God with miracles and wonders and signs which God performed through Him in your midst, just as you yourselves know (Acts 2:22).

Never think sons are a "step higher" than daughters. Sons and daughters are equal in terms of the Lord's blessings.

Let our sons in their youth be as grown-up plants, and our daughters as corner pillars fashioned as for a palace (Psalm 144:12).

This verse mentions sons and daughters, and they have equal roles in the sight of God. God created them, and He has no partiality. The manmade roles may be different for boys and girls in some countries, but from a spiritual sense, there is nothing different between them. The salvation or eternal life is no different for boys as it is for girls. The sons should be "like grown up plants"; not like withered or dying ones. They have to be strong and grown up. The daughters should be "like corner pillars fashioned as for a palace," who stand strong on the principles of God's Word. Sons and daughters have their own unique roles, and they are gifts from God.

8. Do not show Favoritism

Now Isaac loved Esau, because he had a taste for game, but Rebekah loved Jacob (Genesis 25:28).

Never show favoritism toward one child over another. Isaac loved their first son, Esau, and Rebekah loved their second son, Jacob. Isaac and Rebekah were being partial toward their children, and it ultimately resulted in enmity between the brothers. The Edomites (descendents of Esau) and Israelites (descendents of Jacob) were enemies of each other throughout the generations. Parents, it is vitally important to show the same love and favor to all your children. It should not be a case of dividing your love between your children but of multiplying it. When you had one child, you focused 100 percent of your love on that child. When you have two children, it should not be that you give 50 percent to each; they should each receive 100 percent. The love should not be divided but multiplied.

9. Set up your priorities

Parents have to be careful in their priorities. Some parents give more importance to their children than to God. We have already seen how setting up priorities or setting up an order in the home is important.

In the Bible, one man, Eli, gave importance to his sons, who were "wicked" in the sight of God (1 Samuel 2:12–36). God asked Eli, "Why do you honor your sons more than me?" (1 Samuel 2:29) Eli, a priest, being a man of God, loved and honored his sons more than he did God; and it turned out tragic.

We come across many people of God whose children not only do not go to church, they don't have proper fellowship at home. Some children are oblivious when it comes to God and are into worldly things instead. This happens when these men of God are into church activities, and they neglect the family and fail to keep track of what the family members are up to. You have to always be mindful of priorities. Give the utmost prominence to God, and then to your family. Otherwise, your house may be called a Christian home, but your children will not be called true Christians.

```
            GOD

          FAMILY

      OTHER ACTIVITIES
```

Your first priority should be God. Your personal relationship with God is important. It precedes any other relationship. Then comes your family, followed by other activities. Individual families make up the church. Many people think "church" and "God" are the same. They are not the same. All the "saved" people together compose the body of Christ or church.

He must be one who manages his own household well, keeping his children under control with all dignity, but if a man does not know how to manage his own household, how will he take care of the church of God? (1 Timothy 3:4–5)

King Hezekiah was told to set his own house in order before his death (2 Kings 20:1). He was told not to see the affairs of others, but his own house. Setting your own house in order is important to maintain a Christian home. It does not mean we should not take part in church activities, but we have to balance our tasks and set our priorities straight. Only God can give us the wisdom to balance and handle things.

Some people never get involved in church activities, thinking they will not be able to spend time with their family. People give so much preference to their work and barely consider how that work takes time away from family. There are other things, such as spending time with friends, relatives, online chatting, etc. that take away so much time, and people rarely feel bad about that. Only when it comes to church matters do people feel they do not have enough time to work it into their schedule, that church activities will interfere with time spent with the family. We need to balance everything and make decisions accordingly.

10. CHILDREN

We have seen how parents should teach, train, build up foundations, and set an example for their children. Let us now look into some of the responsibilities of children.

CHILDREN

1. Honor your parents
Honor your father and mother (which is the first commandment with a promise), so that it may be well with you, and that you may live long on the earth. (Ephesians 6:2-3)

2. Obey your parents
Children, be obedient to your parents in all things, for this is well-pleasing to the Lord. (Colossians 3:20)

3. Care for your parents
But if a widow has children or grandchildren, these should learn first of all to put their religion into practice by caring for their own family and so repaying their parents and grandparents, for this is pleasing to God. (1 Timothy 5:4)

1. Honor Your Parents

Honor your father and your mother, that your days may be prolonged in the land which the LORD your God gives you. Honor your father and mother (which is the first commandment with a promise), so that it may be well with you, and that you may live long on the earth (Exodus 20:12; Ephesians 6:2–3).

Children are commanded by God to honor their parents, but they will know this only when taught. If parents do not teach their children to honor them, children will not learn. While it is the children's responsibility to honor their parents, it is the parents' responsibility to teach the kids these lessons from the Bible. There is no age when you stop honoring your parents. Children will always be children to their parents, even after they are grown up. When we become parents, we should not forget our parents. We should remember how our parents raised us while we raise our own children.

2. Obey Your Parents

Children, obey your parents in the Lord, for this is right.

Children, be obedient to your parents in all things, for this is well-pleasing to the Lord (Ephesians 6:1; Colossians 3:20).

When kids are young, the importance of obedience should be taught. Kids should obey their parents right from childhood, and it will be easy to continue as they grow up. The importance of obedience should be strongly taught at home, and they should learn that any kind of influence from friends or classmates or other kids should not affect their behavior toward parents. Obedience toward parents pleases the Lord. It is right in His sight. The Bible says that obedience is better than sacrifice in 1 Samuel 15:22. If we do not know how to relate to God and parents through obedience, the sacrifice of praise and worship to God cannot be pleasing to Him.

3. Care for Your Parents

If any widow has children or grandchildren, they must first learn to practice piety in regard to their own family and to make some return to their parents; for this is acceptable in the sight of God (1 Timothy 5:4).

Paul uses the phrase, "Repay their parents and grandparents." Do you think we can ever repay our parents or grandparents for all the love, sacrifice, and hard work they put in while bringing us up? We actually realize the great effort and sacrificial love of our parents when we grow up and have our own children. When we become parents, we understand how much our parents took care of us, and what parental concern means. We can never measure their love and repay them, but all we can do is show our love, gratitude, and honor toward them. It is ok for a son or daughter to say, "Dad, I am thankful for you," or "Mom, I am thankful for you."

11. Grandparents

Grandparents play an important role in bringing up their grandchildren in the ways of the Lord. Grandparents have the experience and have seen their children grow up and give rise to another generation. Gray hair means wisdom and experience. Proverbs 20:29 says, "The glory of young men is their strength, and the honor of old men is their gray hair."

Parents, especially new parents, have no experience raising children, but grandparents have seen it all and have experienced each and every thing the new parents are going through.

Parents have the physical strength to discipline a child, but the grandparents have the emotional and mental strength to impart wisdom to the child. Nowadays, most parents do not have time to spend with their children. What a blessing to have godly grandparents who teach lessons from the Word of God, and pray with the grandchildren and impart the godly heritage. Salvation is not hereditary, but Christian living is. What a great blessing and joy it is for Christian grandparents who brought up their children in a Christian home and are now helping their children bring up their grandchildren. The Christian principles, when shared with children and grandchildren, will be passed on through generations. The Christian principles that have been inherited throughout generations lay a strong foundation for the kids.

In 2 Timothy 1:5, it says, "For I am mindful of the sincere faith within you, which first dwelt in your grandmother Lois and your mother Eunice, and I am sure that it is in you as well." Paul recognized how Timothy's grandmother Lois and mother, Eunice, were responsible for bringing up Timothy as a great man of God. Timothy's grandmother Lois must have been a prayerful lady who set a good example for Timothy to follow. Mother (Lois) and daughter (Eunice) must have set a good example in their talk, relationship, and prayer life. If Lois and Eunice fought with each other over trivial matters, they would not have set a good example for Timothy, and Paul would not have mentioned their sincere faith.

12. Conclusion

A Christian home should have exemplary relationships within the family. All such families make up the church. What joy it would be to see examples set within each family! Children should recognize the importance of parents by considering this acronym for the word **"F-A-M-I-L-Y"**: "Father And Mother I Love You." May our children say such statement wholeheartedly! Children should also be able to say, "Father and Mother say I love you." May parents convey their love to their children in that manner! What a blessing it is to see love for God in the house. That is when the house will be called a Christian *home*. A Christian home is a practical home, one that shows the love and peace of God inside as well as outside.

God bless you and guide you to be a practical Christian balancing relationships with God and family.

About the Author

Benjamin Mittapalli is a seminary graduate from Liberty University with a Master of Divinity (M.Div.) specializing in Biblical Studies, and a Master of Arts in Religion (M.A.R). He is an engineer, with a Master of Science (M.S.) from the University of Maryland. He accepted Jesus Christ as his personal Savior and Lord in 1988 and has been involved in the ministry of the Lord since 1994. He takes active participation in the ministry of Word and prayer, based on his calling from Acts 6:4. He has been involved in church planting, bible studies, prayer meetings, counseling, and youth ministries. He leads Zion Church (www.zion-church.org) in Maryland. He and his wife, MarySalome, and their two children, Jason and JoAnne, live in Maryland, USA.